The wolf is a canine. This means it is a member of the dog family.

The wolf lives in the mountains or places far from cities and towns.

The wolf is a nocturnal animal.
This means it comes out at night
after resting during the day.

Adult wolves live alone most
of the year.

Hunting Club

In the middle of winter, wolves get
together to hunt in packs.

The wolf is an enemy of livestock,
especially sheep.

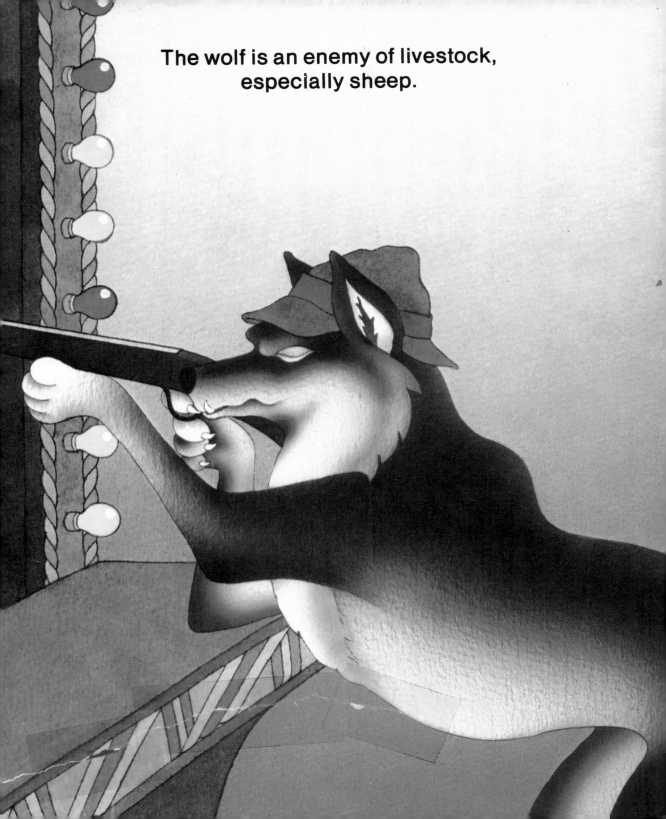

The wolf is a good runner. It can run many miles without stopping.

The wolf is a very smart animal. It can learn many things.

Wolves can be tamed easily if they are captured when very young.

The wolf has been hunted
so much it has almost disappeared.

Each spring, mother wolves have four
to nine wolf pups.